About t

World Poetry Slam Champion 2018, Harry Baker is a poet and a maths graduate. He writes about important stuff like hope, dinosaurs and German falafel-spoons. His work has been shared on TED.com and viewed millions of times worldwide, as well as being translated into over 20 different languages. He lives in Margate.

Details of upcoming projects can be found at <u>www.harrybaker.co</u> or @harrybakerpoet.

Unashamed

Harry Baker

Burning Eye

BurningEyeBooks
Never Knowingly
Mainstream

For Grace.

Thank you for
holding me
in your light.

*Why do something if
you can't be proud of it?*

Kae Tempest

Intro

As I am writing this introduction I have just turned 11,000 days old. I am aware of this milestone because of a poem I wrote as a teenager called 'Paper People'. While I was working on it my mum told me that my grandparents had been praying for me every single day since I was born. I thought this was so incredible that I used to count my age in days and include that exact number in the poem each time I performed it, as a reminder to myself of how often someone had been thinking of me in that way.

When I was 8,396 days old, my grandpa died. I paused the number in the poem as a reference to him, but my 10,000th birthday was already marked out in the calendar as something I didn't want to miss.

My way of celebrating in style was taking a show all about poetry and maths entitled *I am 10,000* up to the Edinburgh Fringe Festival. I was touring this show around the UK up until the point when we decided that crowding in basements wasn't the best idea during a global pandemic, and many of its poems and ideas have become the book you hold in your hands today.[1]

1 — A note on the pandemic: I have tried not to mention the C-word/generally go on about it too much. Partly because it has dominated our lives so relentlessly I don't think it deserves to infiltrate the happy place that is this book, but also I don't know how relevant/like a weird collective dream it will feel to look back on in the years to come. If you are reading this in the distant future (hi!) just know that any reference to being stuck at home/unable to perform is very much down to global circumstances, not because I suddenly got really unpopular for a couple of years.

The show was an excuse to revisit some of the maths I thought I had left behind forever, as well as themes that had always been present in the background of my work. It was enough to give me a renewed enthusiasm to approach maths and poetry together again, and as soon as I scratched the surface I was reminded they had never been that separate for me in the first place. These ideas have helped shape how I see the world, and whether you're a lover or hater of maths and/or poetry, I hope you'll join me in celebrating language, logic and life itself.

Some
Days

Some days
there is a lightness.
When the brilliance
of everything around you
becomes heightened.
When there is
more to life
than indulging your
quarter-life crisis,
and you owe it to yourself
to try and put this down
in writing.

I promise
I will never stop trying.
Even when it's hard to —
I find the prospect
far too exciting.
We forget
the bar we set
has the capacity for rising.
Where it is left
is just the version
we have given up revising.

So this is
HB 2.0.1 (and a half).
Current draft.
The water's running warm,
so pass the bubble bath.
When the going gets tough,
it's tough to get
a dialogue going
that stuff is hard,
but if we come together
there's a chance
we might not come apart.

Whether or not it's growing
on the other half,
the grass is always greener
when you love the grass.
Remind myself
when faced with tougher days
that there are some that aren't;
it might not feel like much,
but then again it rarely does
when it is just the start.

I've never met a second step
as terrifying as the first one.
I've never met another person
there wasn't a chance to learn from.
The more that we spend time
with the uncertain,
the more we can apply
when we revise our current version.

There is a point
when unknown becomes home
and throws you unaware.
When you've been
near the table long enough
to now pull up a chair.
When the place
you knew as new
asks you if you
have cut your hair.
You feel the corners
of your mouth — and soul —
and notice something's there.

Some days
there is a lightness.
When it becomes
all but impossible
to stop the world
from glowing.
There are still
shadows in between
as I wish some days
into most days,
but on those days
I will read myself
this poem.

When
This Is
Over

When this is over,
I will hold you
closer than you've ever known.
When you see me
you can squeeze me
till you feel my very bones.
How I long to let you know
that I won't want to let you go.
There will be so much left to say,
yet still some things are better shown.

I will wrap my arms around you
for the seconds we have lost.
Our words will find a way to wait
as we locate the weight of us.
Though we are changed,
there stays a sense of same
about the way we touch.
Though it is strange,
we will embrace
how long it takes us to adjust.

The world of everything we knew
is somewhere we cannot return.
The world of everything that's new
is one we'll build from what we've learned.
We'd never known ashes could rise again
until we'd seen them burn,
and the next time I stand in front of you
will feel like it's been earned.

When the start has given way,
it's only then the end can enter.
When the heart is given space,
it will forever tend to tender.
These affections kept at bay
can once again descend to centre,
something we'll have come to yearn
as hummingbirds connect to nectar.

For all those overwhelming moments
where I've felt like giving up,
there is no point that I was worried
we'd forgotten how to love.
When the future's all we've got,
well, then that's got to be enough.
All that I know is when I'm low
that I have wanted to be hugged.

And if you'd rather have a handshake,
that is absolutely fine.
Even a wave from me is saying,
I am glad that you're alive.
Whichever form it takes,
when this has passed
and we've started again,
I will no longer take for granted
any chances to connect.

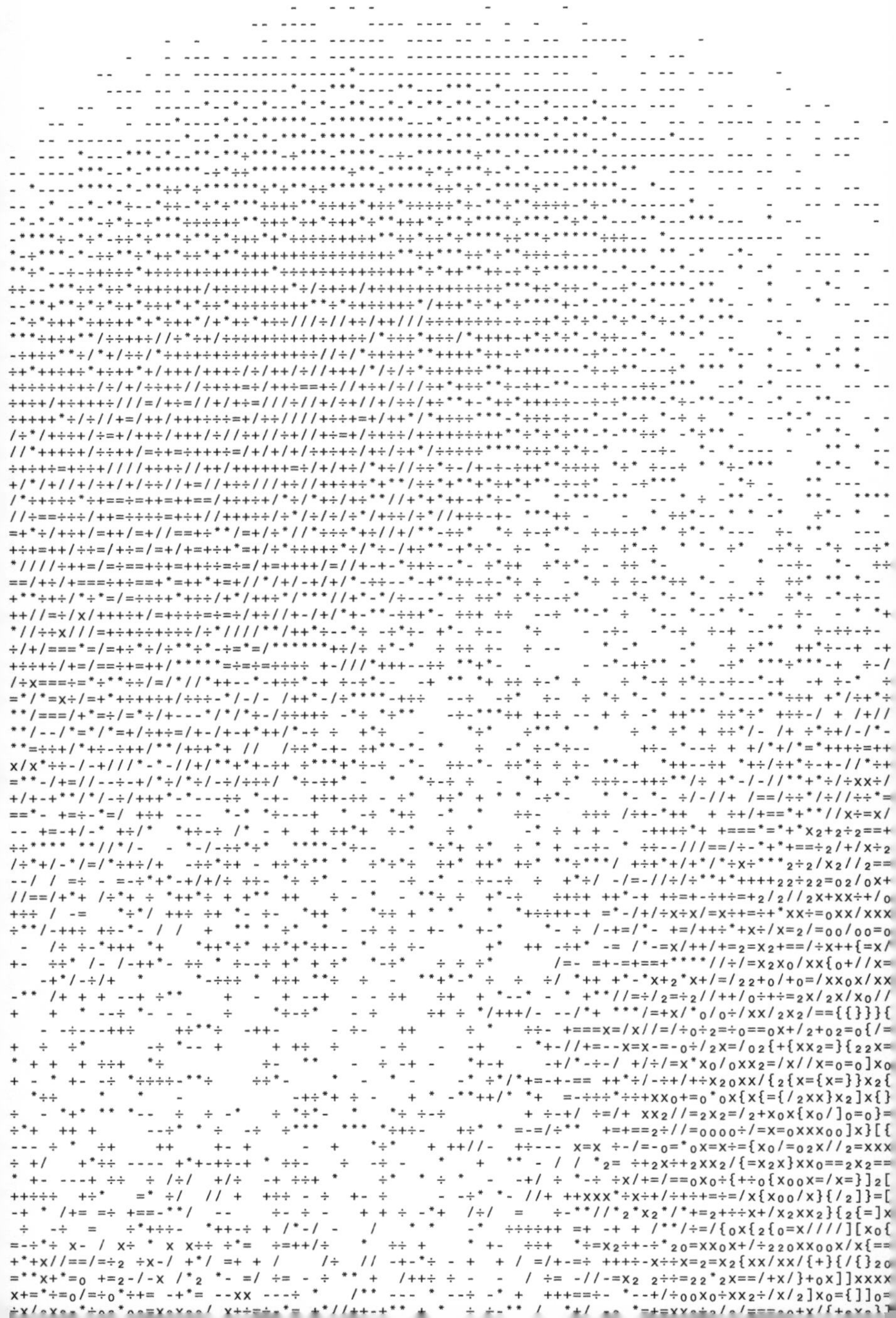

Part One

In summer 2015, having passed my final logic exam by one mark above a fail,[2] I graduated with a maths degree from the University of Bristol, ready to not use that degree in any professional capacity whatsoever. My parents had met at university also studying maths, and, after a brief stint teacher training and analysing submarine rust for the Ministry of Defence respectively, they went on to job-share at a Christian youth work charity — so abandoning maths as soon as possible felt like a family tradition I was only too happy to continue. The part of the path that felt less well-trodden was that I was doing this in order to become a full-time poet.

I had spent four years sitting increasingly confused at the back of lecture theatres, spending more and more evenings and weekends gigging on any stage that would have me when I should have been studying. I was struggling to stay on top of the syllabus, but more pressingly I was often struggling to stay awake. By the end I was mostly ~~dribbling and drooling~~ scribbling and scrawling in the margins of my barely legible notes, certain of what I wanted to do but with no idea of how to go about it or if it would even be possible. I just knew that I had to try.

2 — You could argue that (in terms of efficiency) this is logically the best possible result, but it turns out that is the kind of flawed logic that would only get you one mark above a fail.

I reassured myself that, while others on my course had been doing internships and applying for graduate schemes at Deloitte and Barclays, my equivalent work experience had been getting pennies thrown at me by some teenagers in Swindon I'd mistakenly challenged to a rap battle whilst being brought in as a positive role model. At least if I ever needed a friend who worked in corporate tax loopholes for the inevitable millions I made off poetry, I knew where to look.

While I was in my final year, wrestling as much with the existential question of what to do next as I was with the actual maths questions in front of me, I signed up for the London Marathon — presumably because I felt I had to match this mental anguish with some kind of physical pain. As a poet and a mathematician (two occupations renowned for their athleticism), I did what I assume anyone would do in such a time of hardship and endurance: I tried to distract myself long enough to get through it.

A Mathematician's Guide to Surviving Your First Marathon

Tell yourself the first five miles don't really count.
By the time you get to six,
stay focused on each checkpoint as they come.
6.214 miles and you have made it to 10 k.
6.219 and it's officially 20 miles to go.
6.555 and you are a quarter of the way.
At times when things might feel impossible,
just stick to what you know.

The first step on my literary quest was a three-week bartending course in Barcelona, just in case I needed some transferrable skills to fall back on. Armed with a mixology diploma I have also never used in a professional capacity, I spent half a decade travelling the world sharing my poems,[3] happy in the knowledge that I would never have to scrape through another maths exam again. If I couldn't cut it with the rhymes I could cut it with some limes, and I always secretly expected that when the poetry died down or stopped being fun I might go into teaching, because ~~I don't fancy analysing rust~~ teachers are the best. Yes, I am available for school bookings.

3 —   Followed by a few years where I was suddenly unable to do so, but we'll come back to that.

Except not only has the poetry continued to go surprisingly well,[4] but the maths has very much stuck around too. I'd seen it as a niche hobby I'd reference in the occasional poem, like dinosaurs or pole dancing, just with marginally less scaliness or sweatiness. Yet without the pressure of handing in homework or revising for exams on the sleeper train from Barnstaple, I found myself reading maths books for fun again, and by *again* I mean for the first time. The more I actively sought maths out, the more I discovered my love for it was still there, despite what I had told myself (and anyone else who would listen). Before I knew it, I realised all I had done was graduate from a mathematician-who-also-does-poems to a poet-who-also-does-maths.

Fortunately for both the world and the wider literary canon, before I had this epiphany I was dedicating my energy to writing about important non-mathematical topics such as whether James Bond's name is a grammar mistake and how great my knees are. Let's crack on, shall we?

4 —   This isn't just false modesty; no matter how much I have come to terms with where poetry has taken me, I am reminded that is it surprising by pretty much every hairdresser/taxi driver/smalltalk-loving partygoer I've ever told I make a living from writing poems.

Bond
James
Bond

The name's Bond James Bond.
Bond is both my last and my first name.
For some reason when I introduce myself to people
they think I am repeating my surname.
But if that were the case,
then I would have to say,
The name's Bond, Bond James Bond.

I used to introduce myself to people as Bond Bond,
then they would mishear and repeat back to me, *Bonbon?*
And I would say, *No, thanks — I'm sweet enough.*
And they wouldn't get it.
Then I'd have to explain that it's a bit like Neville Neville.
Then I'd have to explain that that was Gary Neville's dad.
Then I'd have to explain that that was Phil Neville's brother.
Then I'd have to explain who Phil Neville was.
He's a footballer that looks a bit like
the famous poet Harry Baker...

I thought it might make things easier
to start using my middle name,
to see if I could separate
the two Bonds with a James.
But now I wish I'd paid attention
in my A-level chemistry,
because it turns out separating bonds
requires a lot of energy.

I guess it could be worse.
It reminds me of the time I ordered a martini
and, whilst making small talk,
mentioned that my friend Shane cannot stir.

Bond James Bond

Knees

I have incredible knees.
Such is the legend of my knees
that bees use these
as a point of comparison.
When insects come across
a particularly great leaf
or piece of dirt,
they turn to one another and say,
Now this *is the Harry's knees.*

Sometimes
I will catch their reflection
in a shop window
or a puddle
or the tear-filled eyes
of a passer-by and think,
You know what? Yes.

Each time a stranger sees my knees,
they fight the urge to seize my knees.
Campaigns are made to free my knees.
When I die they might freeze my knees.

Ne-Yo
was so sick of love songs
until he saw my knee, yo.

My knees make your knees
weak at the knees.
For my knees, your knees
get down on one knee.
They ask my knees to join your knees
in holy matrimo-knee.
My knees say wait and see.
My knees have been known to tease.

Such is the stress
when my kneecaps lock
that to sufficiently express it
you would need caps lock.

Academics have proposed theses
to make my knees a protected species.
My knees say they don't need protecting, thank you;
they do as they please.
I just have incredible knees.

Websites discuss conspiracy theories
as to whether there exists a miracle knee gene
or if it is more akin to djinn or genies —
if you had three wishes, would you wish for these knees?
Yes, please.

You cannot synthesise
what lies between my shins and thighs.

I've met insurance companies
concerned that I might bump my knees.
They said that they could cover me —
I said your love don't come for free.

Don't ask my knees
to bend and snap;
you know my knees
don't bend like that.

One time I tried
to use these knees
to stunt double
George Clooney's knees,
but a few seconds
through these scenes
he asked to reconvene.
He said they were upstaging him.
I tended to agree.
I just have incredible knees.

Well — I don't just have incredible knees.
They make up the incredible me.

No matter what your shape or size
or what your self-esteem,
whether you're wobbly or knobbly
or somewhere in between,
loving ourselves has to start somewhere,
and so once more I'll repeat:
I have incredible knees.
I just have
incredible
knees.

There is a water station up ahead.
You are almost at mile 7,
which is just a half-marathon away from mile 20,
then it's only another 6 and a bit
until you are allowed to stop.

When I started studying maths at university, I was given the option of switching courses to study maths with a year abroad. Having performed at some poetry slams around Europe previously, I thought it would be an incredible opportunity to ~~make my degree more difficult and ultimately fail my third year~~ live in another country and experience another culture first-hand, so for a year I lived and studied maths in Germany.

As a mathematician and a poet, the German language is the best possible combination; not only is it very logical compared to English, but there is lots of space to be creative in amongst this. One of my favourite ways this occurs is the art of sticking existing words together to make new words, also known as *Zusammenkleben*.[5]

This leads to such delightful examples as a kettle being a *Wasserkocher* (water cooker), a light bulb being a *Glühbirne* (glowing pear), and a glove being a *Handschuh*, because of course — it's like a shoe that you put on your hand. I would get excited about these words and tell my German flatmates it was amazing that they had hand shoes, at which point they would answer, *Yes. We know what gloves are. Why are you so excited about gloves? Do you not have gloves in England?*

5 —   Literally a word meaning to *stick together*, made up of sticking together the words *stick* and *together*. Glorious.

There were, however, other exchange students who would get as excited as me about these discoveries, and we used to message each other our favourite new words as we came across them. This inspired me to keep looking for these compound words out in the wild, and eventually to try and invent my own. Suddenly the idea of learning a new language shifted from something that felt like hard work and grammar tables to something that felt fun and playful.

When I discovered that the German word for falafel is *ein Falafel*, and the German word for spoon is *ein Löffel*, it stood to reason that if you had a specific spoon that you only ever ate falafel with, that falafel spoon would surely be known in German as *ein Falafellöffel*. At this point, how could I not write a poem about a falafel-loving fella called Phil?

Falafellöffel

Phil ist voll.
Die Nacht ist gut verlaufen.
Phil sieht ein Geschäft und er fragt was sie verkaufen:
(Phil is full.
The night has gone well.
Phil sees a shop and he asks what they sell:)

Falafellöffel. Für Löffelvoll Falafel.
(Falafel spoons. For spoonfuls of falafel.)
Was?
Falafellöffel. Für Löffelvoll Falafel.
Wie?
Falafellöffel! Für Löffelvoll Falafel!
Phil doesn't speak German, so he's left a little baffled...

See, there's this fella, Phil.
And Phil loves falafel.
In a falafel raffle
he would snaffle all the tickets.
He always answers in affirmative
to offers of falafel,
even if he's awfully full;
he'd feel awful if he didn't.
For us it might feel effortless
to live a life falafelless,
but Phil effervesces
unless he gets his falafel fix.
So if Phil were ever to be offered
Löffel of Falafel,
he'd say yes despite not knowing
what the eff a Löffel is.

For Phil a life of love and laughter will have a falafel after,
so it's yes despite not knowing what the eff a Löffel is.
If a falafel fell off a Löffel, Phil'd feel awful;
still it's yes despite not knowing what the eff a Löffel is.
A fluffy falafel is often iffy, if he's honest,
yet it's yes despite not knowing what the eff a Löffel is.
If half a Löffel of filthy falafel is overly lethal,
even as we leave Phil he'd still have a message for his kids:
saying yes despite not knowing what the eff a Löffel is,
always yes despite not knowing what the eff a Löffel is.

Call and response:

*Wie viel Falafel ist
zu viel Falafel?*

(How much falafel is too much falafel?)

*Vier Löffelvoll Falafel
ist zu viel Falafel!*

(Four spoonfuls of falafel is too much
falafel!)

*Wie viel Falafel ist zu
viel Falafel?*

*Vier Löffelvoll Falafel
ist zu viel Falafel!*

Vier Löffelvoll Falafel ist zu viel Falafel
if it left him on his deathbed
with a message for his kids:
saying yes despite not knowing what the eff a Löffel is,
always yes despite not knowing what the eff a Löffel is.

Phil war voll.
Die Nacht war gut verlaufen.
Phil sah ein Geschäft
und er fragte was sie verkaufen:
Falafellöffel. Für Löffelvoll Falafel.
Falafellöffel? Für Löffelvoll Falafel!?
Ja — Falafellöffel! Für Löffelvoll Falafel!

You've got to make an effort when you travel.

Get to 7.5 miles and there's only 30 k remaining.
At 8 miles make a joke to yourself about Eminem.

Halfway through my year of ~~eating too much falafel~~ studying in Germany, I was asked to come back and speak at a TEDxExeter event. As a student whose most impressive recent achievement was now having two languages I could struggle to understand maths in, I felt ~~entirely~~ slightly out of my depth at the speakers' dinner the night before, sat between a man who 3D-printed prosthetic limbs and a woman who had decided she was going to walk to the North Pole a year after having triplets. I consoled myself that I was the light entertainment in amongst a collection of both serious and seriously impressive speakers.

Nevertheless, I wanted to give the best performance that I could, because there were 400 people in the audience, and I knew it was being filmed and put online, which would take the total audience up to at least 401. I had enough time for three poems, so I decided I would build my set around my most impressive world-slam-winning 'Paper People' poem, as well as ending on a personal fave, 'The Sunshine Kid', which I would go on to name my first book after.[6] I figured I should therefore probably open with a fun one about dinosaurs to win the crowd over/give them a chance to reset their expectations after whoever had gone before me.

6 — Available at ~~all good bookshops~~ www.harrybaker.co.

I was pleasantly surprised when I got to the rehearsal and not only was I given a lanyard that said *Speaker* on it, but furthermore one of the first things the organiser asked was if I was going to do my poem about prime numbers,[7] because that was her favourite. I hadn't imagined maths to be as instantly crowd-pleasing as dinosaurs, but I still had a soft spot for the first proper poem I'd ever written. Either way I wasn't about to pass up a specific prime-number-poem request, as, much like the prime numbers themselves, you can never be too sure when the next one is going to turn up.

7 —   '59', available in *The Sunshine Kid* at ~~all good bookshops~~ www.harrybaker.co.

Soon you will have made it to 13 kilometres.
This means that if kilometres were miles
you would pretty much be at the halfway point already.
This means the real halfway point
is just 1.6x your current distance,
meaning you are 5/8ths of the way there,
meaning you are 5/16ths of the way to the total distance.
Tell yourself not to dwell on the fact
that 5/16ths does not feel like very much.

One year later and I'm back in Bristol when I receive an email saying that of all the independent TEDx talks, mine had made it into the 0.02% that get chosen to be showcased on the main TED site, and therefore likely seen by far more than 401 people. This was the first point since winning the world slam when I let myself feel the certainty that being a full-time poet might actually be possible.

They went on to say that, because it was now going on the main site, they would make a few small edits to the initial video. This seemed reasonable, and I wondered if those edits extended to cutting out some audaciously chosen mustard yellow trousers that I haven't worn since, or disguising the fact that for a confidence boost I had asked my flatmate James to cut my hair a few days beforehand.[8] It turns out the main editorial choice was going to be changing the title from 'Grand Slam Poetry Champion' to something more appealing for a broader TED audience.

8 — James had no hairdressing experience, and when we met in Fresher's Week he possessed one of the worst haircuts I've ever seen in my life, but I still thought this would be better for my confidence than risking another professional hairdresser asking me what I was going to do after university if the poetry didn't work out.

As this was a time of peak clickbait, I was amazed when the title they settled on was 'A Love Poem for Lonely Prime Numbers'.[9] Not only was this poem a last-minute addition to the set, it was also now the headline event, and instead of an elaborate TED-style description of me as a linguistic dreamscaper or prime rhymologist, the site simply stated I was a performance poet and maths student. They figured that people would want to watch this not *despite* there being maths and poetry involved, but *because* of it.

Within a day this became the most viewed performance I had ever given and therefore the lens through which most people became familiar with my work. Despite having as many poems referencing unicorns as I did maths at this point, I have thus far never been introduced as the magical horse poet (no matter how many times I've insisted upon it in my rider).

Given that I'd written this prime number poem when I was 17, when I turned 25 it felt only fair and square to attempt another number-loving follow-up. I wanted to explore a different kind of love to the angsty teenage pining I had refined over many years, and at the very least it was a chance to indulge in some more maths puns, this time squeezing in as many square number references as I could along the way.

9 —   As opposed to 'You won't BELIEVE how many P sounds this boy with weirdly bright trousers and a terrible haircut can fit into 3 minutes!'

49

49-year-old man, not exactly well-rounded.
Always tried to leave everything as he found it.
Things could be nice and neat with the stuff he controlled;
it only ever got messy when there were others involved.
His hobbies included his N64 —
he'd been tempted by GameCube but wasn't quite sure.
With his Shreddies, he'd go through sudoku each morning
and by night could binge-watch a boxset till dawn.

She was 72. She'd heard time after time
as a woman that she should be well past her prime.
But just last year she'd thrived, hitting 71,
and next year again she'd enjoy proving them wrong.
She grew up in a house of 4 brothers.
As young as 16, she had looked after others,
remembering what her mum said about numbers:
When one does what one does, one can cause wonders.

In his flat things were neatly aligned on the shelves.
He didn't just follow rules, but he liked them as well.
He realised at this point in life that he felt
it was easier spending these times by himself.
Half her lifetime ago, she'd been in his position:
a square that's too scared to step outside the box.
She realised at this point in life that she figured
you squeeze what you can out the time that you've got.

She knew that she needed a plan.
Some way to go about reaching the man.
Given his nature, she'd have to start slow,
but with squares it's amazing how quickly things grow.
9 o'clock the next morning, Shreddies in hand,
he noticed the note as it entered his flat.
Her tentative plan from the previous night
laid out in her neatest handwriting. It read:

We could live out our lives as two parallel lines
or we could find the right angles to meet.
So if you're in need of a decent square meal,
how d'you feel about dinner next week?
These 36 words left him speechless at home.
A yearning was stirred somewhere deep in his bones.
Once seeds have been sown, if you leave them alone,
sometimes all they need is a reason to grow.

This was the meal that she chose:

She preheated the oven, 360 degrees,
almost 361 — it would flicker between.
No need for a main, instead just four sides —
all equal length in their preparation time.

Homemade ravioli, so carefully cut,
laid out on some toast she had spared of its crusts.
A packet of noodles she'd subtly warmed,
although not heating up long enough to lose form.
Four 3×3 waffles, arranged in a grid,
topped with fake plastic cheese on a savoury tip.
She cracked out the crackers and, there in a box,
some squares she had got of some various choc.

As he took it all in, he was so overwhelmed,
he had no idea how to show how he felt.
As if words weren't enough in this space to just be,
all she made him agree was the same time next week.
This became their routine, and his straight edges softened
with Battenberg, baklava, ice by the cube.
The thing with breaking down squares is that often
it just takes some effort to find the right route.

And food is a miracle, to those who would share it.
All it takes is faith in the ones who prepare it.
Whether for a few or 4,900,
when one does what one does, one can cause wonders.

One day as they ate, what he'd stored up inside
found a way to escape in the warmth of the silence.
He said, *I'm so grateful, but have to know why
it was me of all people you chose to show kindness.*
She smiled, and said, *Think of this jelly we hold.
There's so much potential that's yet to unfold.
Somehow only when we let it dissolve
can it spill out, and fill out the rest of its mould.*

And so it was so, such that 72's
seed of friendship she'd sown exponentially grew.
Though I guess there were clues that, collectively summed,
they'd always find a way to connect 1-2-1.
So they kept it 100 — their strength was in numbers;
together there's nothing that they couldn't do.
When one does what one does, one can cause wonders;
even more so, raised up by the power of two.

Concentrate on the giant carrot
that has just overtaken you.
Challenge yourself to keep it in eyesight
for the next half a mile.

The French poet Paul Valéry once said, *A poem is never finished, only abandoned.*[10] While I appreciate the comment on the ever-changing nature of existence and the futility of striving for perfection in art, as a mathematician what I appreciate more is things wrapping up in a neat and satisfying way. At this point the previous poem didn't quite feel finished, but I wasn't about to abandon it either.

For those of you checking off the squares as you go along, you absolute ~~nerds~~ beauties will have hopefully spotted we made it up to 121 and beyond, with the notable exceptions of 25 and 81. Yet hold on to your square hats (mortarboards?), because at this juncture the poem is... 81 lines long! What a time to be alive.

Even if we take the line count to mean 81 is now included (which we definitely do), we are still missing 25, the crucial age that inspired the poem in the first place. To remedy this without disturbing our carefully crafted 81-line setup, our literary loophole is a further 16-line epilogue, at least giving 25 a chance to get involved. Perhaps if Paul Valéry had been able to finish his quote rather than abandon it, he may have gone on to say, *A poem is never finished, only abandoned... unless you come back and finish it like a complete legend.*[11]

10 —   Except presumably in French.

11 —   Or, as he would say, *une légende complète.*

Fast-forward nine months, she'd turned 73,
once again in her prime like she'd said she would be.
He's about to hit 50, he's having a do —
she'd convinced him by saying she'd handle the food.

Which left only the question of the guest invites.
Whether his 25-year-old nephew might attend the night.
He recognised in him the need to fit into place;
it is incredible the difference a year makes. It felt like

half a lifetime ago he'd been in his position,
a square that's too scared to step outside the box.
But he realised at this point in life that he figured
even if a door seems closed you might as well knock,

or at least post a note in a well-chosen moment.
When words can melt walls, well, it seemed only fair
that he'd carefully chosen to share what she'd showed him
and wrote in *P.S. Be there or be square.*

This will take you to the 8.73 mile mark.
This is approximately 1/3rd of the total distance.
This means once you do this distance again
it will just be this distance till the end,
and you know you can do this distance
because you have just done it.
Plus 1/3rd feels way bigger than 5/16ths.

As well as getting to celebrate exciting number-based milestones (of which there shall be more, fear not, gentle reader), another phenomenon that has started to happen more at this stage of life is ~~having to try and explain my job to mortgage providers~~ people I know getting married. Thankfully, not only did I meet someone I wanted to spend the rest of my life exploring the power of two with, but Grace just so happened to propose to me six hours before I was planning to do the same. Yes, please.

When we got married we moved to marvellous Margate. Whereas I can do what I do from pretty much anywhere, Grace had quit her job and was looking for something new when we moved down. When an opening came up in the local ice cream shop, this felt like a great opportunity to ~~get free ice cream~~ meet new people. As I was ~~bored and we didn't have any friends yet~~ taking a break from gigging, I offered to write Grace a poem to hand in with her job application, in an effort to help her to stand out from the crowd.

While I am almost certain that teenage angst has fuelled far more poetry than newlywed bliss, I was also aware that a couple of ~~hundred~~ times Grace had ~~pointedly~~ lovingly asked when I was going to write a poem about her.[12] Naturally, when the moment came for a genuine chance to show my affection through written verse, she ~~jumped at the opportunity~~ reluctantly agreed and handed this in with her application:

12 —   Apparently a seven-minute epic about square numbers and companionship was too left-field, and the seemingly watertight answer of 'you inspire everything I write' raises more questions than answers when the last thing you have written is a poem about how fantastic your own knees are.

Ice Cream Character Reference

There are hundreds and thousands of reasons why
topping the list of applicants happens to be my wife.
Here's the scoop: ever since I got to Feast my eyes
and saw bae, it's baked Alaska — ice cream inside.

She's Fab. There's nothing you need to Twister arm for.
It's legen-dairy how she churns through any problem at the sauce.
So raise a glace — she'll make you laugh like Sofie Häagen-Dazs, or
where other people see Wall's, she sees an open Carte D'Or.

You can see her work ethic raspberry ripple for days.
If she has to work a sundae then she isn't a Flake.
She makes wafer others; when it comes to whipping to shape,
she ain't got 99 problems, so don't listen to Jay.

There couldn't be more of vanilla-gible fit for the job.
It is a Magnum opus every time she opens up shop.
She's been at it since she was Mini: Milking the chances she got.
She can't just manage a little; she can manage... gelato.

I am proud to announce that, four years after handing that in, we ~~now run an empire of ice cream shops~~ still haven't heard back from them. Yet, rather than putting all of our eggs into one ice cream machine,[13] Grace was able to get a job elsewhere, and I am still happily ~~unable to fill in my job on any drop-down form ever~~ carving out a niche trying to find people who might appreciate my wordplay more than a specific ice cream shop on the south-east coast.

13 — Exactly the sort of behaviour that suggests it's a good thing we don't run an ice cream empire.

Once you get to 10 miles
you will have made it double figures.
By 10.488 you will have got to 2/5ths.
Reminisce on how the words *two fifths*
sound like the word *toothpicks*
if it was said with a mouthful of toothpicks
where your tooth is.

I haven't always been this comfortable in my nerdiness. There are a number of reasons for this evolution in my character arc, a big one being learning to give more weight to the words of people who want to build you up rather than tear you down. Another is simply by virtue of being older. The older we get, the more chance we have had to get used to occupying our bodies and minds, and the more comfortable in those spaces we can be. To put it another way, we have had more practice at being alive.

One unexpected consequence of spending longer on this planet is that I have begun to be asked for advice, something I initially found alarming because in my head I am still very much a child.[14]

A recent request for advice arose when two different mums told me in the space of a week that their child was being bullied at school. They asked if I had any advice for them, and wanted to know in particular how I had dealt with it when it had happened to me. Naturally my first thought was, *Why would you look at me and assume I would be bullied at school?* although one of the mums in question is my aunt, so to be fair to her she did have some inside info.

14 —   To give you an idea of what I mean by this, at the time of writing I had genuinely had the remains of a Colin the Caterpillar cake for both breakfast and lunch, and it wasn't even close to my birthday.

She was talking specifically about my cousin, who is completely amazing in every way but who was going through a rough time. I remember, when you are being picked on or experiencing something similar, the temptation is to try to rationalise it.[15] You feel like it must be your fault for some reason, that if only you'd tried harder to fit in it might not have happened. In reality it's something that happens to all kinds of people for all kinds of reasons, almost always more to do with the person doing the bullying.

I wrote this for my cousin, for a younger version of myself, and for anyone who's ever been made to feel small in any way, especially for being 'different', because it takes us a while to work out that's a fantastic thing to be. It's trying to answer some of the questions that I know I at least had at that age, about why it might be happening to me.

15 — Despite maths teaching us that the root of things can often be irrational!

Maybe

Maybe it's 'cause they don't understand you.
Maybe it's because they do and they're afraid of what they see.
Maybe it's because you are not normal.
Maybe normal's not the thing you need to be.

Maybe today will be a good day.
Maybe today feels like it's way too close to call.
Maybe one day you will look back and laugh at this.
Maybe one day you will not look back at all.

Maybe it feels like it's getting harder.
Maybe you're still waiting
for that day to come around.
Maybe it's because I'm a Londoner
that I believe you can't stop building bridges
just 'cause one is falling down.

Right now this feels like everything.
Right now it always is.
It's only afterwards that we can see
there's more than this.
You can be informed by this
without being formed by this.
Just as a calm before the storm,
there is a dark before the dawn in this.

Whoever told you you must shrink to fit in
got their filter wrong.
We are not sculptures to be chipped away,
but platforms to be built upon.

If somehow this changes you,
let it be in a resilience
in knowing that you made it through.
Do not give them an inkling
of a thicker skin.
If we stop listening,
how can the truth that permeates
start sinking in?

Not every day's a battle.
Not every part of life's a war.
It is the times that lie between
that need to be worth fighting for.

Remember what this moment is.
You may not have chosen this,
but one day you will be someone who rose from it.
When you see the same in others
you can notice this,
so show them this:
there's no eclipse
without some kind of glow in it.

Those that know you
know to love you.
Those that love you
love to know you.
Those that don't —
they forfeit the right
to get to be the ones that mould you.
If you ever meet the old you,
say *I come from what you go through;*
there will be times
when that is all you have to hold to.

There will be times you cannot help but cry,
and times you cry for help.
There will be times that you resist
or are too tired to rebel.
When it takes everything
to not just be defined by someone else,
you can start by showing kindness to yourself.

Maybe

Toothpicks.
Toofpiff.
Tooffiffs.
Two fifths.

You'd be amazed at how much distance
you can travel whilst you do this.

Silence

I have this friend called silence.
It felt awkward when we met,
although I've noticed recently
I've started calling them a friend.

I rarely saw them in the city;
our paths didn't seem to cross,
which means the time they spent with me
I learnt to love for what it was.

We never used to get along —
I used to find them too intense,
but when you give somebody time
you'd be surprised how close you get.

And, while I still make baby steps,
they have known me since I was born;
I've just not always recognised them
when they hold so many forms.

And yet still when we are in groups
I see them start to fade away,
and yet still when we are alone
I see they cannot be escaped.

They can be awkward silence —
the type we don't know how to act around,
so we try to distract ourselves
and pretend they're not there.

They can be thoughtful silence —
where I give up what I can't take,
they make room for head and heart-space
when there is nowhere else to share.

They can be awesome silence —
when the world leaves us astounded,
sound can't begin to wrap around it,
so it doesn't dare to try.

There is the warmth of silence —
if we listen they invite us in.
The second we have time to give,
then they begin to thrive.

Silence

And yet still when we are in groups
I see them start to fade away,
and yet still when we are alone
I see they cannot be escaped.

They have been with me in my loneliness,
whether or not I noticed it.
They're with me in my hopefulness,
whether or not I notice this.

Just because you don't see someone
doesn't mean they don't exist.
I know I'm not alone in this.
I know I'm not alone in this.

They lie awake with me at night.
They sit with me when I can't sleep.
They are there when I'm bent double
and can't find the words to weep.

Sometimes we even pray together;
they do not have to say a word,
but every time they're near
I know there is a chance that I'll be heard.

Soon it's 42% of 42 km.
Then it is literally anything you can think of
to make it to halfway.
Once you step past this point
it would technically be further for you
to turn around and run back to the start,
so you may as well just keep on going.

Rescheduled

This wasn't how we pictured this.
It definitely wasn't when.
But the best part of
best-laid plans laid bare's
the chance to start again.
The who is almost what it was.
The where's not quite the same.
For all that's happened in between,
the why remains unchanged.

When they told us we couldn't do this,
we heard we couldn't do this *then*.
When they said it's not possible,
under our breath we muttered *yet*.
Unless it meant something to us,
we would not have fought for this.
The fact that we are here at all
shows how important it all is.

This is not some shoddy sequel;
it's a bangin' remix.
We have had time to crystallise
and realign what we believe in.
If anything, the first time round
was all too easy.
It's not what any of us wanted;
it has become what we all needed.

When this was under threat
we did not run the other way.
We stood our ground
and we announced,
It will get done another day.
For us the question wasn't if or when,
simply a case of how.
The joy of not doing it then
is that we get to do this now.

The race may be named for the hurdles,
yet we celebrate the jumpers.
The storm may come, but in amongst it
we're the ones who hold the compass.
We only hibernate through winter
so we get to see the summers.
This has come over us all,
yet we won't let it overcome us.

Rescheduled

It's not the hiccups we remember;
it's how long we held our breath.
We'll cling that much closer to life
for having come closer to death.
We will be softer, and laugh longer,
when it comes to this attempt.
For, as they say: first the
disrupted-by-a-global-pandemic,
second the best.

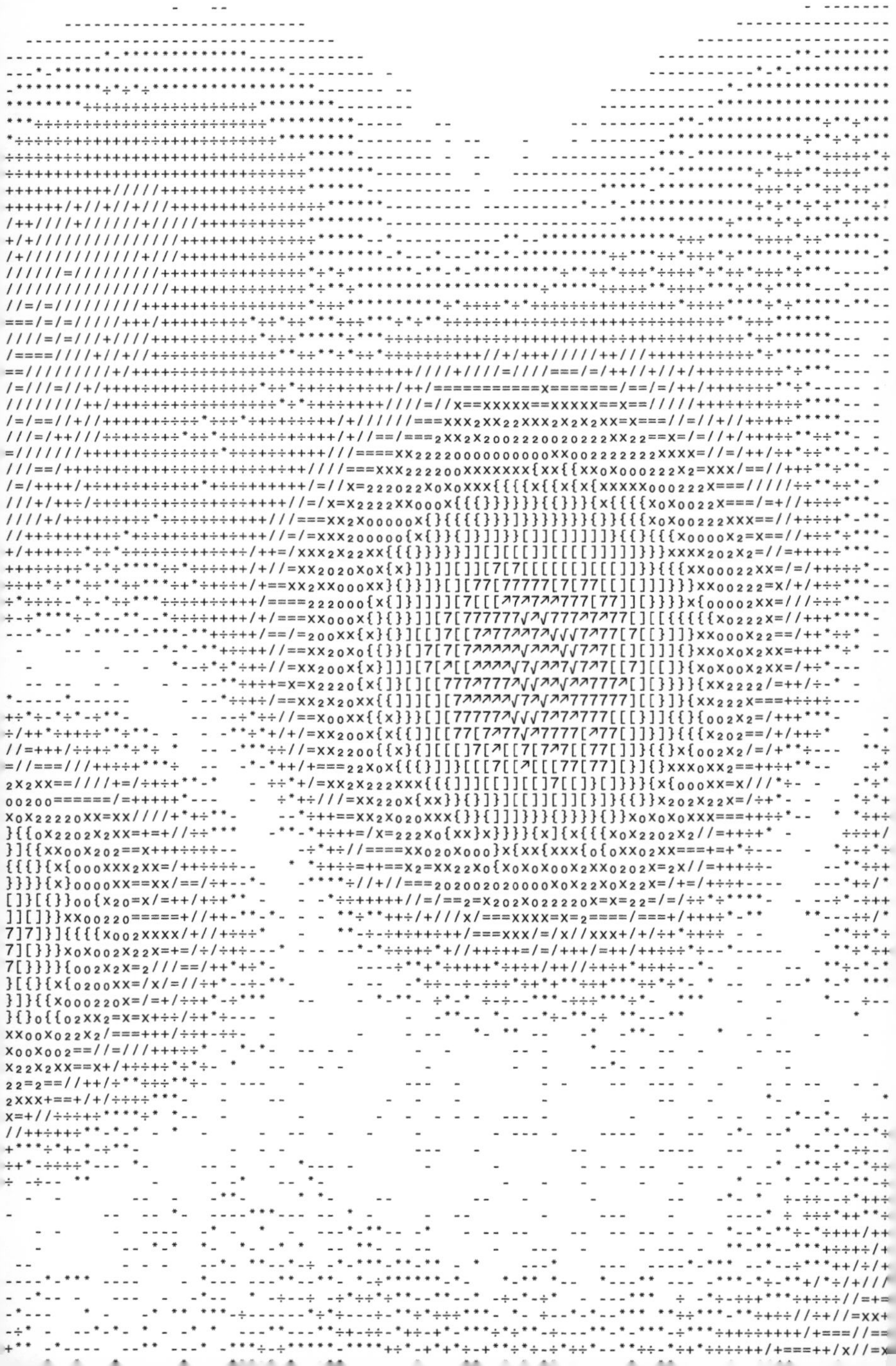

Part Two

Notice how the *15 mile* banner
looks like the words *I Smile.*
How I am way too tired to smile,
but I do smile.

On 16 March 2020, I was invited to perform at an event centred around poetry and climate change in Bristol. With something as massive as climate change it can be easy to feel insignificant or powerless, and with that comes a question of what difference we as individuals can make (if any!). Which I get. But I am also a firm believer in the power of people, and I think a surefire way to diminish that power is to convince ourselves it's not worth trying and give up before we've begun. To quote a Harry and Chris lyric[16] written after one such conversation with a friend:

They say it's just a drop in the ocean,
as if that's a reason to stop.
But maybe they've forgotten the ocean
is entirely dependent on drops.

One of the first poems I ever wrote was about a bumblebee being able to fly despite a scientist supposedly having proven otherwise. Time and time again there are examples in nature where it is not an individual's ability or potential that is limited, but our own imaginations.

Taking inspiration from how often the world hasn't given up on us, I wrote 'Impossible' to remind myself that we don't have a right to give up on it (or ourselves!) just yet, no matter how difficult things may seem. Because, while impossible has a very clear definition as a mathematician, one of the joys of also being a poet is the chance to dream beyond that.

16 — Quoting my own lyric not only feels like an incredibly baller move, but for copyright reasons it is also far easier to get permission from myself than someone else.

A few hours before the event was due to take place, it was announced we were going into lockdown in the UK. A lot of those feelings of helplessness in the face of a huge unknown threat to our existence felt immediately transferrable to what followed. Yet not only was I was heartened and reminded of the collective power we hold by the way individuals came together to look out for each other,[17] but it turned out I needed a poem about not giving up in the face of adversity as much as anyone.

17 —   And the fact that you can just stop pretty much all flights overnight; who knew?

Impossible

I'm finding it too easy
to tell myself it is too hard.
When facing the end,
that it's too late to even make a start.
But if we take impossible
to mean that we don't have a chance,
we have lost sight of how unlikely
it was we would get this far.

The way the single fish
outwits the shark
by sticking with its school.
They way the crescent moon
outspins its dark
to once again be full.
Even winter,
given long enough,
begins to lose its cool.
That which was once exceptional
now barely registers at all.

Flamingos and giraffes
look like they were drawn by a child.
We can't begin to comprehend
all of the ways this world is wild.
None of them asked if they were possible
before they came to be.
None of them have ceased to exist
by being told they're make-believe.

The bug who finds it all too much
and tries to shut off everything,
to recover and then summon up
the strength to stretch its wings.
The snake so full of itself
that it cannot help but shed its skin.
Or how, instead of death,
the hedgehog went to bed
and slept till spring.

To think the Earth exists
at this specific distance from the sun.
Down to the angle of the axis
on which everything is spun.
The fact that trees happen to breathe
that which we need inside our lungs.
It would all seem impossible,
had it not already been done.

We are impossible
to everyone who's ever gone before,
and everyone who's yet to come
will push impossible some more.
Just as indeed the dos we did
outdo the don'ts we didn't,
so everything's impossible
until it isn't.

The thought of rivers changing course
before somebody gave a dam.
Or that the tide might turn from shore
before a line's drawn in the sand.
We cannot know how far our actions go,
the impact they might have.
Sometimes the only thing that we can do
is to do what we can.

Just as the night is at its darkest
when it's introduced to day.
Just as the dry is at its harshest
in the breath before it rains.
It's easy enough to believe in something
when it's all okay.
It is when times are at their hardest
that it's hardest to have faith.

Yet when the light begins to fade,
that's when we need it the most.
It's by surviving day to day
that we see seasons evolve.
If there was never any doubt,
there'd be no reason for hope.
It could be too late to do anything —
it sure as hell is if we don't.

I am tired of the doom and gloom
and self-fulfilling prophecies.
I am trying to find room to bloom
and self-fulfil the opposite.
When it's an act of revolution
to try to stay remotely positive,
there's nothing wishy-washy
about opting to be optimists.

Whether a brighter future's possible
we may not truly know,
but the first step towards that future
is imagining it so.
So as indeed the dos we did
outdo the don'ts we didn't,
so it remains impossible
until it isn't.

When it's over, and we're no more
than old bones within the ground,
still the soil knows to grow its seeds
from what is broken down.
What is lost is always lost
until the moment it is found.
These things only ever go one way
unless we turn them round.

We are so constantly surrounded
that it's easy to forget
this world was built upon impossible;
that has not stopped us yet.
So yes, indeed the dos we did
outdo the don'ts we didn't;
it only stays impossible
until it isn't.

They say *smiles* is the longest word
in the English language.
Because there is a mile
between the two Ss.
They have clearly not come across
the word *shmarathons*.
As in *marathons shmarathons* —
something I only used to say
before I attempted a marathon.
Not only does *shmarathons*
have a full marathon between the Ss,
there is also a rogue H
that somehow got lost along the way.

Today I am very much that H.

When the opportunity to perform live on stage disappeared overnight, one thought was that this would be a great moment to write that second book that the world had been ~~occasionally asking about~~ clamouring for. Yet being unable to do the thing that brings me joy and meaning and a massive sense of my own identity took more of a toll than anticipated. This meant that putting added pressure on myself to finish a huge creative project was not ideal for my mental health, particularly when almost all of my creative (and general) energy was going towards ~~starting a podcast and making sourdough bread~~ simply getting through each day.[18]

What felt more manageable was focusing on smaller things. I opened up a commissions page where I wrote bespoke poems for people's birthdays and weddings (and pregnancy announcements!). I worked with my brother to design prints that could go up on people's walls, so that, while I couldn't share them in person, at least my words could reach others another way. When we got a new toilet seat (genuinely one of the highlights of the year) and I was asked if I wanted to leave a review online, I took that to be a direct invitation to share my thoughts in verse. I wrote a poem about missing hugs and discovered lots of other people were missing hugs. I tried to remain optimistic the fourth time my tour got rescheduled. I swam in the sea. A lot.

18 —   When I write it like this it feels obvious, but it honestly took me two years, a terrible first draft and a good few months of therapy to figure this out. While this was undeniably a difficult time for a myriad of reasons, if you want a clue that this part of the story has a happy ending, you're holding it in your hands!

When you were only allowed to meet up with one other person outside to exercise, my friend Jessie and I made a pact that we were going to swim every single day throughout winter. This meant that on the days when nothing else felt possible, at least we had achieved something. It became not just a reason to get up in the morning, but an urgent and necessary reminder of the thrill of being alive.

Wild

I've never regretted going for a swim.

Even on the days
I have almost talked myself out of it.
When the warm duvet
clings to me like seaweed.
When on the way
the wind whispers,
It's not too late to turn back.
When I am stood on the edge
and shivering
before I've even begun.

Deep breath.
Feet clench.

And yet the second I am in
it is all worth it.
Okay — five seconds after I am in
it is all worth it.
Somehow every single time
it still surprises me how cold it is.

My technique is
less Wim Hof,
more grunt like warthog.
Flail limbs underwater
until things begin to warm up.

When the cold hits you,
it becomes impossible
to think about anything else,
and this year of all years,
that is not nothing.

Jessie is my swim buddy.
We both went
every day through lockdown 2.
We've carried on in tier 3,
even more in tier 4 —
at least they can't shut down the sea.

Jessie is hardcore.
Like, proper puts her face in.
Like, casually brings up
doing a 5k race in conversation.
Barista-trained, she brings a Thermos
and spare mug for coffee after.
I think it's honestly
the greatest thing I've ever tasted.

I love how much
I do not need to be the best at this.
Each day the fact I'm in at all
is an achievement,
and this year of all years,
that is not nothing.

Whether it's
wetsuit with the hands and feet
or swimsuit with a beanie hat.
A full-on lap,
a there-and-back,
often not even that.

The safeword is *stiff chewing gum.*
As in the texture that your muscles feel
when they are begging you to get out.

Even through winter,
we've met fellow swimmers
every time we've gone.
Exchange a brief hello,
an *ooh, it's cold,*
or simply just The Nod.

Realise how much this year we've bonded
through a shared sense of complaining,
whereas here the default setting becomes
Isn't this amazing?

Whether grimacing or grinning,
you can see it in our eyes.
Skin is pink and we are thinking,
What a time to be alive.

Wild

A dog-walker on the way home
chuckles, *Rather you than me.*
I can't help smiling to myself
and think, *I rather do agree.*

As the feeling teases
back into my fingers,
stood in the shower,
waffles and sausages
heating up in the oven,
I am already looking forward to tomorrow,
and this year of all years,
that is not nothing.

My legs are currently hotter
than they have ever been.
I don't mean sun-hitting-the-skin heat;
I mean coming-from-within heat.
It's as if centuries of central heating's
entropy has entered me.

It's at this point the mind descends
to senseless centring on centipedes.

Like how if there was a centipede
that measured just one centimetre
and you gave that to me
to forward to your friend called Peter,
that's a centimetre centipede
that's sent to me to send to Peter.

Toilet
Seat

When people say be kind to yourself,
they can forget to tell you how.
It's more an overarching vibe
than something grounded in the now.

But there is more to life than yoga
or a mindfulness retreat.
If you want to practice self-care,
buy yourself a toilet seat.

You see, a toilet's more than just a place
to empty your intestines.
It's a safe space. It's a haven.
It is somewhere to invest in.

It's where I have my best ideas.
It's where I catch up on the news.
Epipha-wees, e-poo-phanies
I'll later share with you.

And so I'm all for scented candles,
but for something more concrete,
if you truly want some me time,
buy yourself a toilet seat.

I considered glow-in-the-dark
for midnight trips without the light on.
I thought of one with fish in it,
then thought those fish might end up frightened.

Instead it's graphite grey. MDF.
Soft-closing on its hinge.
It's like a sensei bidding you farewell
when you have done your thing.

It is amazing.
It has revolutionised working from home.
In that moment I'm Khaleesi
sitting on the Iron Throne.

So do you really need that spa day
or that holiday in Crete?
You don't have to find out the hard way;
buy yourself a toilet seat.

It doesn't matter if you're renting;
you can take it when you leave.
If your mental health needs mending,
buy yourself a toilet seat.

The next time you've been well behaved
and you deserve a treat,
remember chocolate melts. And flowers die.
Just buy a toilet seat.

If they came together
just to measure their collective wee,
we'd see the centipede centre peed
essentially a centilitre.
Or, if Jesus let his friend
attempt to represent the species,
we'd see St Peter's centripetal
centipede-y centrepiece.

The irony being
getting obsessed with centipedes
now gives my legs a sense of peace.
At least until we get to mile 17.

The rise of the online gig meant ~~with everyone on mute you could hear my soul being crushed in real time~~ there was no longer a geographical barrier to performance. International school visits were now possible without the Flugscham,[19] so long as you remembered that time zones exist. This led to such exciting situations as me waking Grace up at 7am with a dinosaur shriek directed at some teenagers in Hong Kong, which I think we can all agree is a very romantic way to start a holiday.

Alongside my strict self-care regime of sea swimming and reviewing toilet seats, the main reason I was able to get through the past few years was Grace.[20] In one online session about love poetry where I shrieked like a dinosaur at some teenagers in Kentucky, the students asked if I had written any love poems inspired by my wife. I explained that I had recently finished a cracking poem for her about ~~my knees~~ ice cream, and soon discovered they were as underwhelmed by this heartfelt gesture as the ice cream shop itself. The time had come to try again.

As a teenager my idea of love was that it had to be something massive and unexpected that could knock you off your feet (like a dinosaur!). While I am still a big fan of that side to it, more than ever I have come to appreciate the everyday, consistent nature of it too. This one's for you, Grace.

19 —   Literally *flight shame,* meaning the environmental guilt of travelling by plane, because *of course* the Germans have a word for this.

20 —   Pandemic or no pandemic, I'd like to think this specific sentence will always have some truth in it.

Dust

It's not the flowers;
it's the weeding in the mud with you.
It's not the champagne;
it's the cuppa in that favourite mug you use.
It's not the chocolate;
okay, yes, it is — but not just one or two.
It is becoming
Bruce Bogtrotter and Augustus Gloop.

It's voting frozen pizza
over fancy grub with you.
Because some nights
nothing can beat
a slice of comfort food.
It's knowing anything I eat
will include some for you.
'Cause you're not hungry,
but you might just have a couple spoons.

It's not the dreaming;
it's the waking up with you.
I want to be here long enough
to gather dust with you.

We both agreed
even romantic baths
need bubbles too.
But now I see
maybe the snorkel
was too much for you.
And yes, the submarine
and rubber duck
came out a touch too soon,
and yet the fundamental truth is
I have fun with you.

It's watching crappy films
because that's what you want to do,
then, on the nights you're gone,
finding I want to watch them too.
It's knowing, if it came to it
and I had option to,
I would not change a single thing
of what I've got with you.

It's not the dreaming;
it's the waking up with you.
I want to be here long enough
to gather dust with you.

For us love isn't in the air;
that is just where we found it.
All this is built upon
what we have done to ground it.
It's not the spark when we first met;
it is the lifetime built around it.
It's by small amounts
that mounds amount to mountains.

I need not justify, adjust
or fear I'm judged by you.
Such is the glorious consistency
of loving you.

My heart's not skipped a beat;
it still constantly thuds for you.
Such is the everyday magnificence
of loving you.

It's not something we fell into
so much as stumbled through.
It's the spectacular normality
of loving you.

It's not the dreaming;
it's the waking up with you.
I want to be here long enough
to gather dust.

By this point the gaps between milestones
seem to stretch a little bigger.
By 20 miles you've technically got
to double double figures.
That is like quadruple figures.
That is like 1,000 miles.
That is like I have run 500 miles
and I have run 500 more.

Do anything you can at this point
to not get the Proclaimers stuck in your head.
And, while you're at it,
try not to worry about Mum.

My mum loves running. The main reason I signed up for the London Marathon in the first place was that ~~I was running away from my problems~~ she convinced me it would be a good idea. She devised a training plan for me and, one week before the race, my brother and I went round to my parents' house to drop off my costume.[21] At which point she gathered us in the kitchen and told us she had been diagnosed with breast cancer.

One of the first questions she asked the doctor when she got her diagnosis was *Will I still be able to run?* and she was delighted when on her medical report they included her marathon PB time, because they knew how important that was to her. She worked out that because of the way the cycle of chemotherapy worked, every three weeks she would have had a chance to regain some strength just before getting hit with the next dose. As a way of claiming back some agency when so much of it was being taken away from her, she decided she would try and run to each one of her appointments, with various friends and family joining her along the way. During this time she wrote a blog about her experience, and she eventually turned that blog into a book[22] and asked me if I would write and perform something for the book launch.

21 —   As I was raising money for Amos Trust, who do incredible work in Palestine, I decided to raise awareness by running dressed as a replica section of the Israel/Palestine separation wall, only to find all cameras avoided me because it was considered too controversial. Six years later I ran again with the softer approach of dressing as a giant Falafellöffellaufer (falafel spoon runner), which was somehow deemed to be a lot more accessible.

22 —   *Run for Your Life* by Jenny Baker, published by Pitch in 2017.

I have always maintained that I love maths because there are definite right answers, and I enjoy poetry because there are fewer wrong ones, but there is still a moment when crafting a poem when it just feels right. Whether it is a particularly satisfying rhyme or turn of phrase, when the words slot into place in a certain kind of way, it is as if it is meant to be. Yet for one of the first times ever this didn't happen. I had no idea how to fit this big messy life event neatly into a poem, so I initially focused on coming up with something about running the marathon instead. I was only eventually able to write about Mum's treatment directly when I noticed the word *chemotherapy* has the word *mother* slap bang in the middle of it. From that moment on the poem seemed to write itself.

There Is a Mother

There is a mother in the middle of chemotherapy.
Sitting at the end of reason is a son.
But there's a treat at the beginning of each treatment.
In amongst the brunt of everything — a run.

While Mum was off work to have her treatment, she started a feminist card company (with Grace!) called Out of the Box Cards. She was tired of the limited choices of mostly pink and pretty cards to buy her nieces for their birthdays, and so decided to make some alternatives — what a legend. Alongside their other brilliant ranges they have a series of poetry cards, featuring a quote from a poem on the front with a longer extract on the back, and asked me if they could use my 'Maybe' poem because ~~they knew they wouldn't have to pay me~~ they respect me as a person and an artist. As I was effectively creating a new show all around a special birthday (albeit a slightly more niche one of 10,000 days), in return I asked them if they would be up for creating a bespoke birthday card with me to mark the occasion.

I've always loved birthdays. As a kid it wasn't just the excitement of eating cake, hanging out with friends and getting presents;[23] I also distinctly remember being another year older as something you would look forward to. There were milestones such as reaching double figures at 10, becoming a teenager at 13, or being old enough to ~~buy fireworks~~ partake in democracy at 18. At uni some people would make a big deal about their 21st, but after that it seems we only deem it to be a worthy occasion when we reach a new decade, and some people seem reluctant to even do that. For me birthdays are an excuse to celebrate life, something I think we should do at every opportunity we get. It breaks my heart when people dread their birthday as if it is nothing more than an unwelcome reminder of our inevitable descent into decay and death.[24] Getting older is a privilege and a joy, and I believe we owe it not just to ourselves, but to those who don't get the chance to have another year on this glorious messy planet, to try and make the most of that where we can.

I also love birthdays because they are a chance to celebrate people. And I like people. For one specific day you are able to focus on the joyful fact that a particular person exists, and you have an excuse to tell them that you love them — to their face, or indeed via a birthday card with a quote from their favourite poet on the front.

23 —   Although these are still very much three of my favourite activities.

24 —   This wasn't the quote I went for on my birthday card.

A Birthday Poem

There are roughly 7.7 billion people in the world.
And each one had a day that they came to be.
That's roughly 7.7 billion and one birthdays,
if you count two for the Queen.

Of these 7.7 billion and one occasions,
there's only so many moments
where they can take place.
Over the course of the year,
if we spread out the celebrations,
we're talking 21 million birthdays a day.

That is 900,000 BPH (births per hour).
15,000 Born Every Minute
sounds like a very different show.
We get 4/1000ths of a second
for our own private party,
or share a day with 21 million others
that we may or may not know.

But this is where we come to you.
Of all the 21 million people
in the world that were born today,
that I have met.
You are the best one yet.
You are the best one yet.

If 24 miles is Christmas Eve,
then 25 will feel like Christmas.
By 26 it's almost more impressive
if you don't go the full distance.

What I have come to appreciate that maths and poetry have in common is they are all about patterns and connection. They are both a way of trying to figure out the world around us, be it through literal figures or figures of speech. I have always enjoyed making connections between seemingly random things, and what started out as a fun way to entertain myself and my friends has become a lens through which to process the world.

They are also both inherently playful activities. It was by playing with numbers that I was able to distract myself long enough to complete a marathon, and it was only when I started to try and have fun with the German language that it fully opened itself up to me. Even with more serious subjects there is still an innate sense of joy in trying to craft a poem in the best possible way; it was by playing with words that I finally found a way to write about Mum's treatment. One of the many ways the pandemic affected me was that I could feel myself losing that sense of wonder, and now that it is coming back I am hanging on for dear life.

This poem came from a place of playfulness. I wanted to mess about with alliteration again, but instead of ~~getting obsessed with falafel~~ just sticking with one sound, I would go through the whole alphabet and pick something for each letter, which in turn became a gateway to trying to map the history of the universe as I went — just to keep it light.

Given that I could have chosen anything in existence, I need to include a disclaimer that for the letter P, I went for a Peperami. This is because the percentage of pork in a Peperami is 108%. That means for every 100g of Peperami, 108g of pork has gone into it; it has lost weight in the process. While as a mathematician this is clearly a flawed measuring system (and as a vegetarian it is extremely worrying), as a poet I think it is a wonderful metaphor. They say you should give 110%, and it turns out Peperami have come the closest out of all of us.

Maths and poetry have both encouraged me to pay attention to the world around me. My default setting when I come across new situations is to try to find the beauty in them, to see the world as connected rather than disparate, and I am forever grateful for this. Something as simple as counting my age in days rather than years was enough to shift my perspective entirely. This poem was an effort to shift that perspective further, celebrating the connections not just in language but in everything else that has got us up to this point.

Going forward, I will continue to search for connection wherever I can.

An A-Z of Time and Space

First there was nothing.
I'm talking nothing but nothing.
Then there was something.
In amongst that nothing was something.
And something somehow split into some things,
and some things even managed to become things.

Take Adam. Adam was added up out of atoms.
Before that it was black and barren, then it became big and bangin'.
Out of the chaos came countless crazy complex patterns
and then, dun dun dunnnnn — dinosaurs happened.

Through evolution, everything's edited every day.
That's how we fine-tune, finesse and then finally find our way.
Just as the galaxies had got into gear, the game changed,
because hip hip hooray, *Homo sapiens* came!

We invent, imagine, inspire and innovate.
We've journeyed from jamming in caves to jamming jam in a cake.
The knack for knowledge knitted and knotted away like silent Ks.
We learn the language of living — often a little late.

We make music. We manoeuvre mathematical methods.
We've noticed and noted the nodes of our own neural networks.
Overflowing, outpouring, open mics to operatics,
we are the pork percentage purported on Peperami packets.

We question. From quick quizzes to quantum quarks.
Revolutions of the heart to renaissances of art.
Scriptures and science seek signs of the sublime;
meanwhile through trees trickles the entirety of time.

Our universe is unfinished, but utterly underway.
Its vibrancy vibrates via ventricles, valves and veins.
We wander and we wonder, we explore and we explain.
We yearn for what is yonder as we zoom out into space.

We can forget
that we were not
the first to be here.
By any stretch
we will not be
the last to leave.
Whilst we can't
control our history
or know our distant future,
we can make the most
of what might lie between.

We can be kind,
and we can accept
the kindness of others.
The world shows us
what we allow ourselves
the time to discover.
We can listen — truly listen
to another person's needs,
not just wait until
they've stopped talking
to take our turn to speak.

We can be brave enough
to try and make all kinds of mistakes.
We can be playful,
because what is a life without play?
We can remind ourselves each day
it's not too late for new beginnings
when a single moment
can hold the whole universe within it.

When we zoom out
we realise how small it becomes.
So either none of it matters,
or all of it does.

From
atoms,
Big Bang,
chaos,
dinosaurs,
evolution, the
fine-tuning of the
galaxies to
humans,
imagine that
journey of
knowledge through
language and
music;
nodes
overflow with the
poetry of
quantum
revolution. As the
sublime
trickles through the
universe's
veins, we
wander, e-
xplore,
yearn and
zoom out once again.

When we zoom out
we realise how small it becomes.
So either none of this matters,
or all of it does.

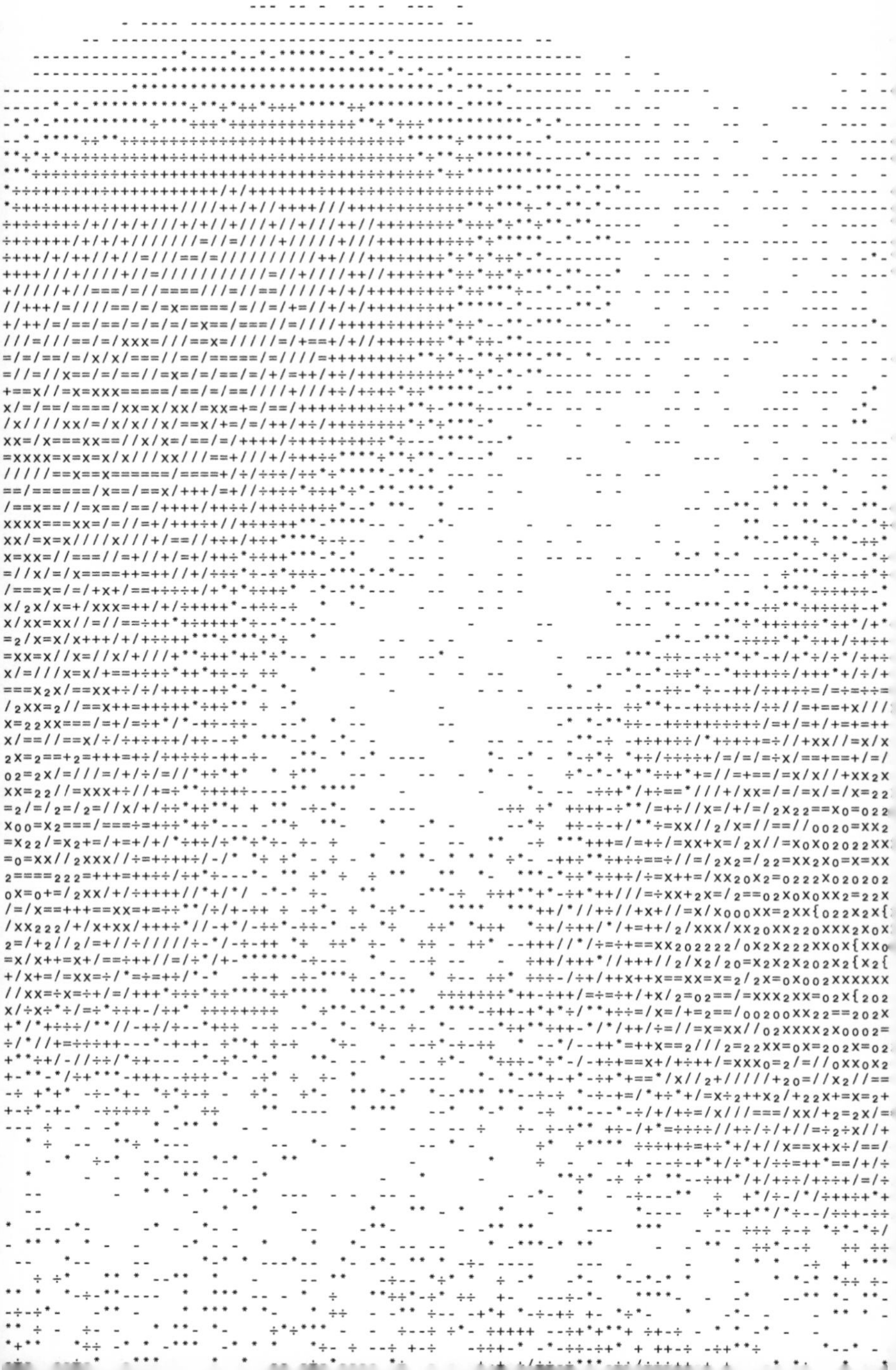

Outro

One of the joys of touring a show explicitly containing maths and poetry was ~~storing up memories for the following two years when I would only be performing to my own computer screen~~ seeing whether audiences had come specifically for one or the other, or (dream scenario) both, or (surprisingly often) neither. It has since led to some deliciously niche gigs, such as being booked as an after-dinner speaker for a conference of tipsy maths teachers[25] or featuring alongside a professional chocolate tasting as part of an online cryptologists' Burns Night event — I guess you could say we both had bars. While I was used to getting nerdy about language with other poets and rappers, it was often more mathematically minded folk who found me after the show to tell me they had also celebrated their 10,000th birthday, and ask if I was looking forward to turning a billion seconds old.[26] These are the same people who celebrate when 14 March matches up with the digits of pi in America, or who got excited when 22/2/22 was not only a palindrome, but also happened to fall on a Tuesday/Twosday. These are very much my people.

25 —   Honestly one of my favourite performances ever.

26 —   To which the obvious reply is *I wasn't, but I am now!*

Yet my favourite response to the show was not from a poet or a mathematician, but my other core demographic: concerned mothers. One mum messaged me the day after a show to ~~ask me how I coped with being bullied at school~~ tell me her 11-year-old son Dougie had come along and been inspired to work out that he was currently 4,208 days old. He was excited by this because he was born on 4 February 2008, and it just so happened that on the one day he looked it up, his age in days precisely matched his date of birth of 4/2/08. Absolute scenes.

His mum said he was so excited that he shared it in his class group chat and the overwhelming response was, *Who cares?* This broke her heart, but she wanted to share it with me because she knew I would appreciate it, and it meant the world to him to know he wasn't alone in thinking stuff like this was cool.

Not only did I appreciate it *so* much, but I thought plenty of others would too. I tweeted this out and asked if anyone else thought it was cool, to which over a thousand people responded that yes, it is obviously very cool indeed. Some even began to try and work out when their age in days would match their date of birth — so many that my brother made a website, www.dougieday.com, where you can type in your date of birth and it tells you when your own 'Dougie Day' will be. Mine is when I'm 53 and I can't flipping wait.

If you carry on like this
you may just make it
to the finish.

The important thing is not to overthink it.

There was a phrase that Dougie's mum used to describe him that completely broke me. She said that he's a really special kid, as *He sees patterns and beauty where others just see nerd.* Not only was that me as an 11-year-old, it is who I aspire to be now, and I desperately hope he is able to hold on to that.

As a teenager (and beyond!) there is so much pressure on fitting in that we can lose some of our weird and wonderful selves along the way. These days I am less concerned with fitting in than filling out. Rather than shrinking or editing down, I believe that it is by encouraging and nurturing the many and varied parts of one another that we can become the best, fullest versions of who we are meant to be.

I have learnt to embrace maths and poetry as fundamental parts of who I am. They are not the be-all and end-all of me, but they have informed the way I navigate this wild and precious life. They have helped me appreciate the connections between my surroundings, as well as giving me a way of forming new connections with others. They have cultivated a sense of wonder at the wider world, as well as that which lies within.

When we give space to the bits that feel like they don't quite fit in, we can celebrate the sum of us and not just some of us. When we can embrace the entirety of who we are, that is when we can feel most alive. And that is surely something worth celebrating.

Unashamed

It's not your job
to make sure others feel more comfortable.
You need not dull your glow
in the hope they might see.
You need not water down your core
to be more palatable.
May you be the you
that you need you to be.

Unashamed.

We cannot help how others see us,
though we may well try our hardest.
How we see ourselves
can free ourselves
to be ourselves
regardless.
Home is where
you can be open-hearted.
Whether trapped or trapeze artists
all comes down to how we're harnessed.

I'm tryna free my roots.
Like playing pass-the-parcel
packed with parsnips.
When the music stops
and no one's watching,
will you keep on dancing?
Let us decorate and garnish
any reputations tarnished,
'cause despite it all
I still fancy our chances.

Let us not file away our edges
in an effort to be smooth
when the records show the dents
are how we get into the groove.
All that energy invested
in the editing of you,
I hope one day you'll let it loose
and let me be there when you do.

In the moments
when your guard slipped
for a second or two,
I could have sworn
I caught a glimpse
and I saw heaven in you.

Unashamed.

The only time I'll know
if you've lost weight
is shedding expectations.
Unless you're Senator Organa,
there's no point adopting layers
when the heart of you's
the part of you
that's blazing.

Others may have tried
to hide your light.
You may have
joined in this yourself.
But, joy of joys,
the joy of joy
is it shall not
be overwhelmed.

You could be static,
or your static
could cause lightning storms.
Whether it's lions or
it's iron ore,
your core contains all types of raw.
That friction that you feel
is an igniting force,
so light the torch.
If we can't see it in ourselves
then what is brightness for?

We do those closest to us
a disservice
if we only ever let them see
the small of us.
If we can open up enough
to let them get beneath the surface,
there's so much more to love
if we can show them all of us.

The flaws in us.
The force of us.
The full-on awe of us.
The rise and fall of us.
The wise and fool in us.
Yes, all of us.

The fine and coarse of us.
The fine print in the clause of us.
The fire imprinted in our blood cells
as they course in us.
It's all in us.

Regrets that haunted us.
The second thoughts that torture us.
The lessons taught to us.
The tightrope life kept taut for us.
It's all for us.

The morning
that seems daunting
till it dawns on us
that there is more adored in us
than simply what's adorning us.

The times others have thought of us.
The times they've fought for us.
Because if anyone's worth fighting for,
of course it's us.
It's always us.

So call it what you want;
there's something calling us.
And I have caught enough of you
to know that you're enough.

Any boxes
they may try and stop you with:
instead of building up a fort,
let's make a rocket ship.
Treat them as photos —
not negatives developed into positives,
but nothing more than
simply a snapshot of things.

All the best bits of your story
are still yet to be unfurled.
You are the caterpillar
that becomes the butterfly
that flaps its wings
to cause an earthquake
halfway round the world.
You are amazing.

And if they try
to rain on your parade,
let it remind you
how much fun it is
to party while it's raining.
May you take up space
and stay there

unashamed.

I think we can all agree that would be the perfect place to finish. But it's my book and I can do what I want, so this final poem is about Christmas.

As a fan of birthdays, I was thrilled to be asked to provide a Christmas meditation for the radio a few years back. In many ways Christmas is the ultimate birthday, not just of Jesus Christ himself but also of the German tradition of Feuerzangenbowle, which involves melting a rum-soaked cone of sugar into mulled wine. What is not to love?

My mathematical interpretation was to look back at my first 24 Christmases on this planet as an advent calendar of memories. I still love to perform this during the festive season, so now, in the ultimate Christmas present to myself, I can do that from my own book, rather than hastily trying to piece it together from scraps of paper beforehand. God bless us, every one.

Christmas
Through the
Ages

1   It's not realising it and yet being the centre of attention.

2   It's being more excited about the wrapping paper
    than the presents.
    It is a box. It is a rocket. It is a fort.
    It is the thought that counts.

3   It's just about grasping the concept of December.

4   It is loving it at the time
    but still being too young to remember.

5   It is the school nativity.
Where you don't have to be the star
to be the star of the show.
Where a tea towel on your head
and a dressing gown combo
will somehow define you
as wise.

6   It's writing Christmas cards for everybody in the class,
because they sell them in packs of thirty
and why wouldn't you want to be friends with everyone?
Being too young for classroom politics.
Being too young for worrying
about how many kisses is too many kisses.
A simple *Happy Christmas* printed in the middle.
Their name at the top, yours at the bottom,
and you can blitz them in a night.

7   It's Uncle Steve dressing up as Father Christmas.
It is Toby's mum ringing up your mum upset
because you told him about Father Christmas.
It's James Mclynn telling you 10 years later
that you told *him* about Father Christmas.
It's finding it hard to believe
you found it so hard to believe
when it came to Father Christmas.
It's wanting to put the record straight today
for all the younger listeners;
the truth about Father Christmas —
is that sometimes he gets my uncle Steve to help out
when things get really busy.

8   It is a joint Christmas *and* birthday present
      for you *and* your brother.
      Four presents' worth of present in one
      in the form of a PlayStation 2.
      Applying a similar concept of sharing
      to your daily half-an-hour time limit:
      the first half-an-hour is Joel's half-an-hour —
      I'm just helping out.
      The second half-an-hour is my half-an-hour —
      but I can't do it without him.
      The third half-an-hour is
      We're just looking for a save point, Mum!
      Twice your current lifetime away
      you will ask Joel about presents growing up
      and this will still be the one that you both remember.

9   It's discussing when you're allowed to get up,
      instead of when you have to sleep:
      Can we come in at six? How about seven?
      Settling somewhere between the two.
      Arriving at 6.01, stockings in arms,
      at the end of Mum and Dad's bed.
      It's a bit of a squeeze now —
      you are both bigger than you used to be.
      Taking it in turns with Joel to go through the classics:
      Selection box.
      Chocolate Orange.
      Chocolate gold coins.
      Pants and socks.
      Shower gel.
      Satsuma.
      Even when you are told you are too old
      for Santa to keep bringing you presents,
      you will do stockings for each other
      and make sure all the above are still included.

10   It's wearing shorts every single day of the year
while you still can,
because when you start secondary school
you will be forced to wear long trousers against your will.
It is Friday afternoon.
Rolling a giant snowball
the entire 30-minute journey home,
kneecaps glowing so red
Rudolph himself would be jealous.

11   It is Year 7 taking snowball fights to a whole new level.
Two pairs of gloves —
one for warmth, one for craftsmanship.
Ringing up school to check in advance
if it's been cancelled for a snow day,
hearing that Drayton Manor School's pipes have frozen —
maybe ours will be the same.
It's organising a meet-up in the morning
on Ealing Common either way.
Arriving sodden into period 3 French —
pardon — sorry I'm late, miss.
There was traffic because of the snow,
which is technically true.
It's her saying that she taught your brother
and she knows you walk to school.
It's somehow still not getting into trouble
because snow rules.

12   It's deciding to go to the cinema
        as a family on Christmas Eve.
        Not knowing this will become a tradition you stick to
        more closely than any mince pies or mistletoe.
        That you will go through that *Napoleon Dynamite* phase
        for slightly too long.
        That you will cry your eyes out
        watching *Where the Wild Things Are,*
        because you too *just want to make everyone okay.*
        Your brother will laugh at you in the kindest possible way
        that somehow only brothers can.

13   It's Beth saying she respects your music taste
        but it is seriously lacking in Christmas songs.
        Making you a compilation of all the classics,
        including Mariah Carey, Destiny's Child and the Tweenies.
        Informing you that S Club 7's
        'Never Had a Dream Come True'
        is still a Christmas song
        because it came out during November
        and it was snowing in the video.

14   It's having to get to church early.
        Mum's been asked to do the Christmas morning sermon,
        to go out live on BBC.
        Five minutes before broadcast,
        you're asked if you and Joel wouldn't mind
        moving from the front row.
        His afro is blocking the people behind
        and your new *Napoleon Dynamite* 'Vote for Pedro' T-shirt
        could be interpreted as a political message.
        You do not want to make a scene before Mum goes up
        but make it your mission to get in the background
        of as many shots as you can.

15 It's doing your paper round on foot
when it's too icy to go by bike.
Being up and awake and getting to make
the first footprints in the snow.
Texting the mates you know will check their phones
before looking out the window.
It's Chris telling you that if you post a note
through each door in early December
you are more likely to get a Christmas tip.
Photocopying a handwritten message
and filling in the gaps for a personal touch:

To the recipients of
the _____ at number ____,

Thank you for the honour of
letting me deliver your papers
each morning all year round.
In these cold winter months
it is nice to have something
to get out of bed for.
Lots of love, your faithful servant
and daily bringer of news.
Harry

16 It's going to midnight mass the night before
so you can have a lie-in on Christmas morning.
Checking the order of service for carols
as soon as you've sat down.
Fingers crossed for 'O Come All Ye Faithful',
because that is an absolute belter,
and hoping for anything other than
'Once in Royal David's City', because:
1 —   it doesn't complement your vocal range, and
2 —   you and Mum refuse to sing that all Christian
        children should be mild and obedient.

17 It's going with Mum to help pick out a Christmas tree.
Last year Dad was in charge and it ended up as
a pile of sticks in a pot with some baubles on top.
Remember to pack your gloves
to carry it back across the common.
Pass the point where in as little as three weeks
these trees will begin to be discarded.
The same point you and your mate Oisin will stop
on the way home from the pub one night,
wondering if that pile of fir is as soft as it looks. It's not.
But, with trousers tucked into socks
and coat zipped all the way up to the top,
arms crossed — you leap back into it regardless.
As you lie amongst the scent of pine
talking about nothing for hours,
there is a freshness to this
that you will look back on
for many years to come.

18

It's finding out your uncle Steve
has an old snowboard in the garage.
If it settles we can definitely give it a go.
It's North Devon turned North Pole.
It is less than two inches of snow.
It's *after you, bro!*
It's broken collarbone.
It's calling his then-girlfriend-now-wife
and her thinking it's a joke.
It's reheated Brussels sprouts after a trip to A&E.
Watching Joel struggle to open his presents
with only one hand,
laughing in the kindest possible way
that somehow only brothers can.

It's using this as an excuse one week later
to get out of a NYE gathering
where the invitees include three other couples,
you and your ex.
Saying *I would love to be there if I can,*
but my brother might need help;
he can only open things with one hand.
Escaping awkward embraces
as the clock counts down to midnight,
choosing board games and hootenanny
with bro and then-girlfriend-now-wife.
It's not quite what I expected as a plan.
It is still the best New Year's Eve that I have ever had.

19

It is doing Christmas together
for the first time as a couple.
She bought you a T-shirt with a dinosaur on it
because you have a poem about dinosaurs.
You bought her a large tub of peanuts
because her brother is allergic to peanuts.
She can't have them at home,
so when she goes out it is always a bit of a treat.
You have no idea just how well you will
eventually get to know each other.
Especially given that you will break up one month later.
You will not be able to stop wearing that T-shirt.
You will question whether or not
the peanuts were a good idea.

20

It's Grandma starting a competition
on Mum's side of the family:
who can make the best stocking/bauble/place mat/tree.
We gather around Grandpa's bed so he can judge.
People have spent months on this.
Mum will always knit something.
Dad will try and subvert the idea
of what it is we are trying to make.
Uncle Darren's will probably involve
some kind of welding.
Me and Joel will have made ours
in the car on the way up.
When youngest cousin Carrie wins
Grandpa will be accused of favouritism.
It is hard to know who is joking and who isn't.

21 It's living in Germany and realising they do Christmas
so much better than we do.
Learning a Schokowerkzeug is literally
a spanner made of chocolate.
Learning a Marzipankartoffel is genuinely
a blob of marzipan decorated like a potato.
Learning that Glühwein really does
make your insides glow.
Feuerzangenbowle is the same
but with extra rum and fire involved.
You will try to bring this last tradition home with you.
Misinterpreting the ratios will leave Great Auntie Pauline
passed out in front of the fire.
This Christmas you will speak
more words to her in German
than you have in English
for the last three combined.
The next year her gift to you
will be a suitcase for your travels
that will keep going on adventures
even longer than she does.

22 It's a second chance to do Christmas together
for the first time as a couple.
She buys you some dinosaur-shaped chocolates
because she knows how much it winds you up
still being given themed gifts for a poem
you wrote five years ago.
You buy her anything but peanuts.

23   It's volunteering to cook vegan Christmas dinner this year
because of Mum's treatment.
You've never cooked a regular Christmas dinner before,
so you may as well give it a go.
It's paper hats and Christmas crackers
and there is no turkey in sight.
Celebrating on the 23rd this year —
you tell yourself it is okay to break some traditions.

Last year was your first
Christmas morning away from Joel.
This year will be your first
Christmas Day away from Mum and Dad.
It's being especially grateful for family this year,
and ever thankful you have Grace to hold your hand.

24   It is taking the time to go back through
every Christmas you've ever had.
Realising in amongst everything else changing
there has been a constant throughout:
that you remember the presence of individuals
more than individual presents,
except for the PlayStation 2
you and your brother got when you were eight.

It's one year since Mum's been given the all-clear.
It's a unanimous decision
that this year's film will be *Star Wars*.
It's still dairy-free but maybe the occasional pig in blanket.
It's asking Grace if she remembers the peanuts
the same way you do.

It's your niece not realising it
and yet being the centre of attention,
knowing as she turned one this year,
she still has everything ahead of her,
knowing as you turned 24 this year,
you still have everything ahead of you.
It's praying that she won't grow up
to be mild and obedient.
It is promising that you will be ready
to answer the call from Father Christmas,
in case he needs Uncle Harry to help out
when things get really busy.

It's still keeping your fingers crossed for
'O Come All Ye Faithful' on Christmas Day,
but packing your headphones in your bag
for the journey home just in case.
It's being grateful for your blessings,
just as Chance the Rapper said.
You made it through this far;
are you ready for what's next?

Acknowledgements

With thanks to my maths teachers:

To Mrs Dickinson, who said she was relieved when I made mistakes because it showed I wasn't a robot.

To Mrs Frith, who valued kindness over cleverness.

To Mr Arthur, who burnt me three days' worth of hip-hop CDs after he saw me rapping in the school cafeteria.

To Mr Massey, who would teach us two months' worth of syllabus in one lesson, so he could get on with the more interesting stuff.

To Mr Palfreyman, who still sends a monthly maths puzzle to ex-students, which I will gladly drop everything to try and answer first.

To Misha Rudnev, who encouraged me to go to the Poetry World Cup even though it could have clashed with end-of-year maths exams.

To Roman Schubert, who, when I needed a pass mark of 50 to be allowed to go on my year abroad, gave me an overall mark of 50.1.

To Hannah Fry, Simon Singh, Matt Parker and Alex Bellos, who helped me to fall in love with maths again as an adult.

To Emma, for making maths fun even when it wasn't fun.

To Dougie, for seeing patterns and beauty where others just see nerd.

Plus an honorary English teacher:

To Ms McMeel, who saved us all.